THE WISH CARD RAN OUT!

by James Stevenson

GREENWILLOW BOOKS • New York

Printed in the United States of America.   First Edition.   1 2 3 4 5 6 7 8 9 10

Library of Congress Cataloging in Publication Data: Stevenson, James.   The wish card ran out!   Summary: Charlie tries to undo the last wish made on a charge card from International Wish, a corporation which has taken over fairy godmothers and wishing wells, but the company has gone out of business.   [1. Wishes—Fiction.   2.   Cartoons and comics]   I. Title.   PZ7.S84747Wi   [Fic]   80-22139
ISBN 0-688-80305-9   ISBN 0-688-84305-0 (lib. bdg.)

For Ava

..MAYBE I DID THE WRONG THING...

WELL, THANKS FOR TRYING, MR. RUFUS!

WHAT DO WE DO NOW, SPALDING?

AT THIS POINT, CHARLIE, I'M FRANKLY BAFFLED.

HEY, YOUNG FELLA! YOU MIGHT SPEAK TO DAPHNE..

WHY?

WELL, SHE USED TO BE A FAIRY GODMOTHER.

COME ON!

EXCUSE ME, BUT WE HEAR YOU'RE A FAIRY GODMOTHER!

I'M RETIRED.

THE COMPANY GAVE ME THIS JOB WHEN THEY TOOK OVER THE WISH BUSINESS.

COULD YOU GIVE US THREE WISHES?

I'VE GOT FLOORS TO DO.